BIZET

CHILDREN'S GAMES
(Jeaux d'Enfants)

Opus 22

MMO CD 3043
MMO Cass. 404

The See-Saw
(L'Escarpolette)

GEORGES BIZET
(1838-1875)

The See-Saw

(C'Escarpolette)

4

Spin The Top
(La Toupie)

Allegro vivo ♩ = 152

SECONDO

Spin The Top
(La Toupie)

PRIMO

Allegro vivo ♩ = 152

8

The Doll
(La Poupée)

The Doll
(La Poupée)

The Merry-Go-Round *

(Les Chevaux de bois)

Allegro vivo ♩. = 152
Sempre non legato

SECONDO

f   di _ mi _ nu _ en _ do   mol _ to   p   cresc.

sf   p

cresc.   sf   cresc.   f

p   dim.   p   cresc.   sf

The Merry-Go-Round

(Les Chevaux de bois)

MMO CD 3043
Cass. No. 404

Badminton
(Le Volant)

Andantino molto ♩ = 60

SECONDO

Badminton

(Le Volant)

MMO CD 3043
Cass. No. 404

Bugler And Drummer

(Trompette et Tambour)

SECONDO

Bugler And Drummer
(Trompette et Tambour)

Soap Bubbles
(Les Bulles de Savon)

Soap Bubbles
(Les Bulles de Savon)

PRIMO

MMO CD 3043
Cass. No. 404

28

Puss In The Corner
(Less quatre coins)

SECONDO

Puss In The Corner

(Less quatre coins)

Blindman's Buff
(Colin-Maillard)

Andante non troppo quasi andantino ♩ = 68

SECONDO

Blindman's Buff
(Colin-Maillard)

Andante non troppo quasi andantino ♩ = 68

PRIMO

Leapfrog
(Saute-Mouton)

Allegro molto moderato ♩= 116

SECONDO

Leapfrog
(Saute-Mouton)

Playing House

(Petit mar, Petite femme)

Playing House
(Petit mar, Petite femme)

The Ball
(Le Bal)

The Ball
(Ce Bal)

PRIMO

BIZET
CHILDREN'S GAMES
(Jeaux d'Enfants)
Opus 22

MMO CD 3043
MMO Cass. 404

MUSIC MINUS ONE 50 Executive Boulevard • Elmsford New York 10523-1325